TRUE
Identity

The Radical Reclamation of the True Self through 12 Reflections from Nature

DAWN RICHERSON

Art&Soul

True Identity
*The Radical Reclamation of the True Self
through 12 Reflections from Nature*

Art + Soul Books
An Imprint of Creative Revolutions Inc.
Dawsonville, GA

Featuring photographs from the Radical Reclamation Series
and the Nature of Life Collection of photos "from the soul for the soul"
by Dawn Richerson Photography

ISBN 978-1-942969-66-2 e-book
ISBN 978-1-942969-67-9 print

Printed in the United States of America

WEBSITES
DawnRicherson.com
DawnRichersonPhotography.com

Table of Contents

Introduction

THE PHOTOGRAPHS IN THIS BOOK are from the Radical Reclamation Series and the Nature of Life Collection, which offer an exploration of what it means to come fully to life and live in full expression by connecting to our core truth. These photographs from nature and the reflections that accompany them comprise the "True Identity Project." This project and the series of photos "from the soul for the soul" came about through the exposing of lies that have too long obscured from me my own true identity and kept me bound by cycles of shame and suffering.

The True Identity Project is an intensely personal exploration of my own reclamation of a stolen or shattered identity—something that has plagued me for the better part of my life but in a most subtle and destructive way in the 20 years between 1997 and 2017. I trust that sharing my own return to seeing rightly and a restoration to my soul's deep knowing of its home in God will reconnect you to your essential story of life. The intent of this project was to provide an evocative and in-the-moment interpretation of new truth statements about my identity as a child of God.

I first had the idea for this project and exploration around 2012, sketching a few loose thumbnails for paintings that would explore the nature of our identity and accompany the affirmations of true identity I had written many years ago. But the sketches stayed in a folder until something in me was crystallized in November 2018 and I had the fresh inspiration to pair the reflections with photographs from nature.

While I had previously identified these false beliefs as a part of my long healing journey, this process showed me the degree to which these lies had continued to steal something precious from me. Suddenly, I could see the cunning and collusion of an array of malignant, misguided beliefs which had kept me off my path, spinning in circles.

It is my deep honor and privilege to share my exploration with you and to invite you to consider your true identity as a child of God. You and I have come to experience life and life to the full. You deserve to know yourself as you are known in the heart of God, as pure and innocent, belonging wholly to life and meant to come more fully to it.

Thank you for allowing me the opportunity to share with you. My books, paintings, and photographs are an invitation to the dance of your life. I hope they open a sacred conversation that will bring you back to life in all its wonder and grace. My desire for me, you, and our world is for life and life more abundant, possible and predictable when you embrace your essential self, journey, and truth. My these simple seeds for life reconnect you to your true identity and to your essential story of life. I'm happy to be on the way with you! DAWN RICHERSON

@dawnrichersonart *Instagram, Facebook*
@dawnrichersonphotography *Instagram*

I Am a Shining Light

Once I believed a lie. I believed that I was a failure.

I believed my light had been extinguished, snuffed out, that it was too late for me, that I had nothing at all to offer. I believed it when the Prince of Darkness whispered to my broken spirit that I would never meet success or a friend who believed in me.

Once I believed a lie. But now I know the truth of my identity.

The Spirit of the Living God has breathed a fresh wind of promise upon my life. I was blind, but now I see. The truth has been revealed: I am a shining light—a gift of grace to myself and to all the world.

Set free from the chains of a lie that bound me, I am restored to true identity.

True Success

"Last Light Upon the Waters"

The Nature of Life Collection

Radical Reclamation Series • True Identity Project

I Am an Integral Part of the Whole

Once I believed a lie. I believed that I was a misfit, belonging to no thing and no one, adrift and alone in time and space.

I believed I could never fit in and would never be accepted if I showed my true colors. I believed it when the Prince of Darkness whispered to my broken spirit that I was too far gone to be brought back, too close to the fire to not be consumed and turned to ash.

Once I believed a lie. But now I know the truth of my identity.

The Spirit of the Living God has breathed a fresh wind of promise upon my life. I was blind, but now I see. The truth has been revealed: I am an integral contributor to the body of Christ and to so many circles of belonging here and now.

Set free from the chains of a lie that bound me, I am restored to true identity.

True Belonging
"Family of Humanity"

The Nature of Life Collection
Radical Reclamation Series • True Identity Project

I Am the Calm Within the Storm

Once I believed a lie. I believed that I was troubled and disturbed.

I believed it when they called me crazy and said I needed to be caged. I believed it when the Prince of Darkness whispered to my broken spirit that I had lost all capacity and would never know this thing called peace.

Once I believed a lie. But now I know the truth of my identity.

The Spirit of the Living God has breathed a fresh wind of promise upon my life. I was blind, but now I see. The truth has been revealed: I am at home within my still center, and there I am at peace. I am filled with grace and truth. I am the calm within the storm.

Set free from the chains of a lie that bound me, I am restored to true identity.

True Peace

"I, of the Storm"

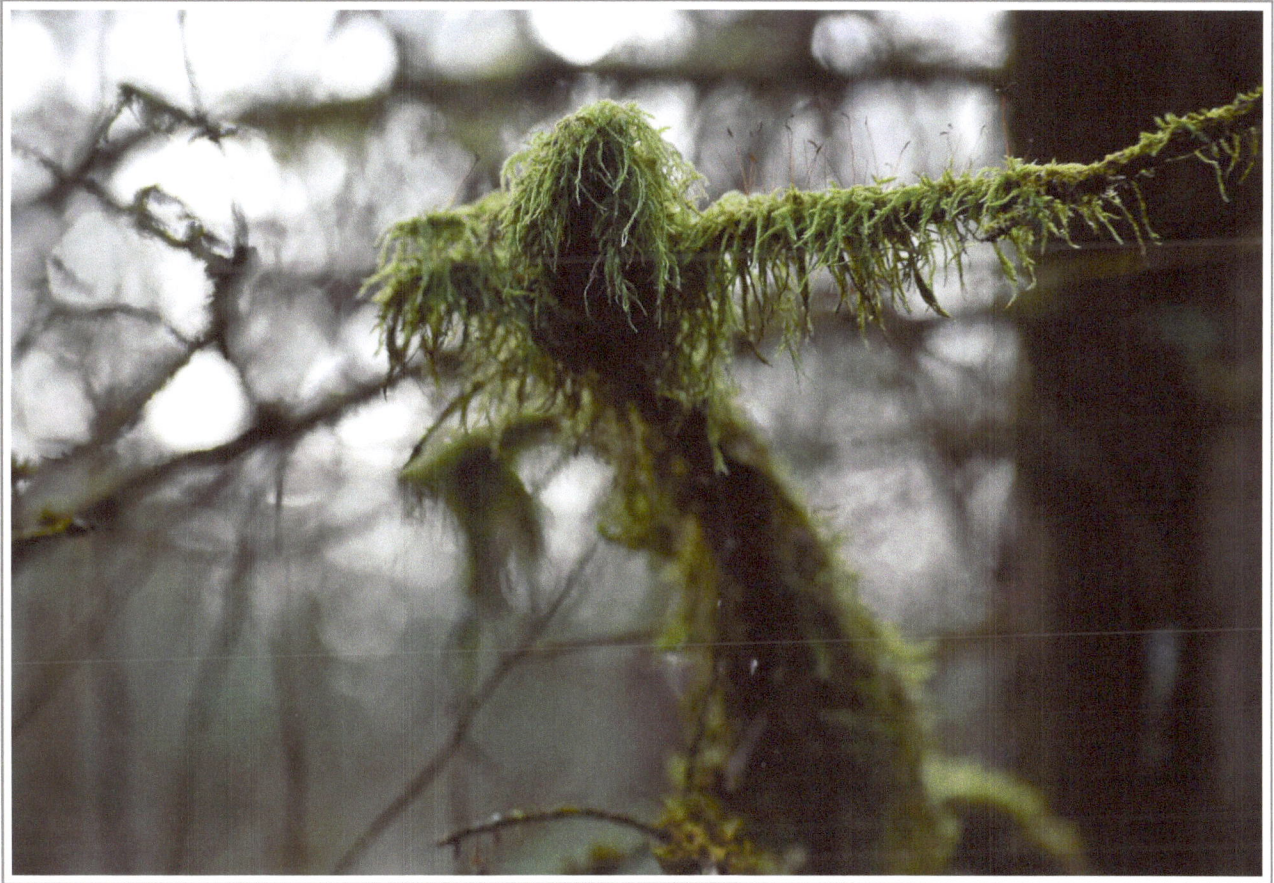

The Nature of Life Collection
Radical Reclamation Series • True Identity Project

I Am Knowing, Known by Heart

Once I believed a lie. I believed that I was slow and stupid.

I believed I just didn't get it and likely never would. I believed my brain was broken beyond repair. I believed it when the Prince of Darkness whispered to my broken spirit that my mind was a black hole filled with endless chaos and confusion.

Once I believed a lie. But now I know the truth of my identity.

The Spirit of the Living God has breathed a fresh wind of promise upon my life. I was blind, but now I see. The truth has been revealed: I am wise and able to take swift action in response to my heart's clear knowing.

Set free from the chains of a lie that bound me, I am restored to true identity.

True Wisdom
"The Gathering"

The Nature of Life Collection
Radical Reclamation Series • True Identity Project

I Am Uniquely Beautiful

Once I believed a lie. I believed that I was weird.

I believed I was deviant, so far out of the range of acceptable to be stamped out and marked "invalid." I believed it when the Prince of Darkness whispered to my broken spirit that I would always be discarded and that I brought only death and decay.

Once I believed a lie. But now I know the truth of my identity.

The Spirit of the Living God has breathed a fresh wind of promise upon my life. I was blind, but now I see. The truth has been revealed: I am uniquely beautiful, stunning in the ways my contributions matter to many. I am a true original.

Set free from the chains of a lie that bound me, I am restored to true identity.

True Originality

"The Angel Who Gave Me Back My Heart"

The Nature of Life Collection

Radical Reclamation Series • True Identity Project

I Am Loved as I Am

Once I believed a lie. I believed that I was unlovable.

I believed it when I heard them say if I ever said this or did that, that would be the end of any hope for love. I believed it when the Prince of Darkness whispered to my broken spirit that I was beyond the reach of love.

Once I believed a lie. But now I know the truth of my identity.

The Spirit of the Living God has breathed a fresh wind of promise upon my life. I was blind, but now I see. The truth has been revealed: I am loved beyond measure for the whole of who I am, and I am one with Love and God.

Set free from the chains of a lie that bound me, I am restored to true identity.

True Love
"Conviction"

The Nature of Life Collection
Radical Reclamation Series • True Identity Project

I Am a Minister of Reconciliation

Once I believed a lie. I believed that I was a harbinger of death who brought irreparable harm to those I loved.

I believed my very being, my essence true and pure, was corrupted to the core—that I was rotten and a poison to the world. I believed it when the Prince of Darkness whispered to my broken spirit that I would be lucky the day I died when, finally, I would no longer hurt the ones I loved.

Once I believed a lie. But now I know the truth of my identity.

The Spirit of the Living God has breathed a fresh wind of promise upon my life. I was blind, but now I see. The truth has been revealed: I am a minister of reconciliation called forth to bring healing to the nations by daring to make the twin journeys to sacred wholeness and soulful transformation.

Set free from the chains of a lie that bound me, I am restored to true identity.

True Healing
"These Tears We Have Spilled"

The Nature of Life Collection
Radical Reclamation Series • True Identity Project

I Am Held in Love

Once I believed a lie. I believed that I was cursed to an eternity of lostness.

I believed I would walk through the desert of forever alone, with danger lurking everywhere. I believed it when the Prince of Darkness whispered to my broken spirit that I would never have a moment's rest, much less be restored to anything or anyone.

Once I believed a lie. But now I know the truth of my identity.

The Spirit of the Living God has breathed a fresh wind of promise upon my life. I was blind, but now I see. The truth has been revealed: I am found as I walk in the way of my life, held in love and an infinite grace, met along the way with blessings unimagined.

Set free from the chains of a lie that bound me, I am restored to true identity.

True Grace
"Oasis of Infinity"

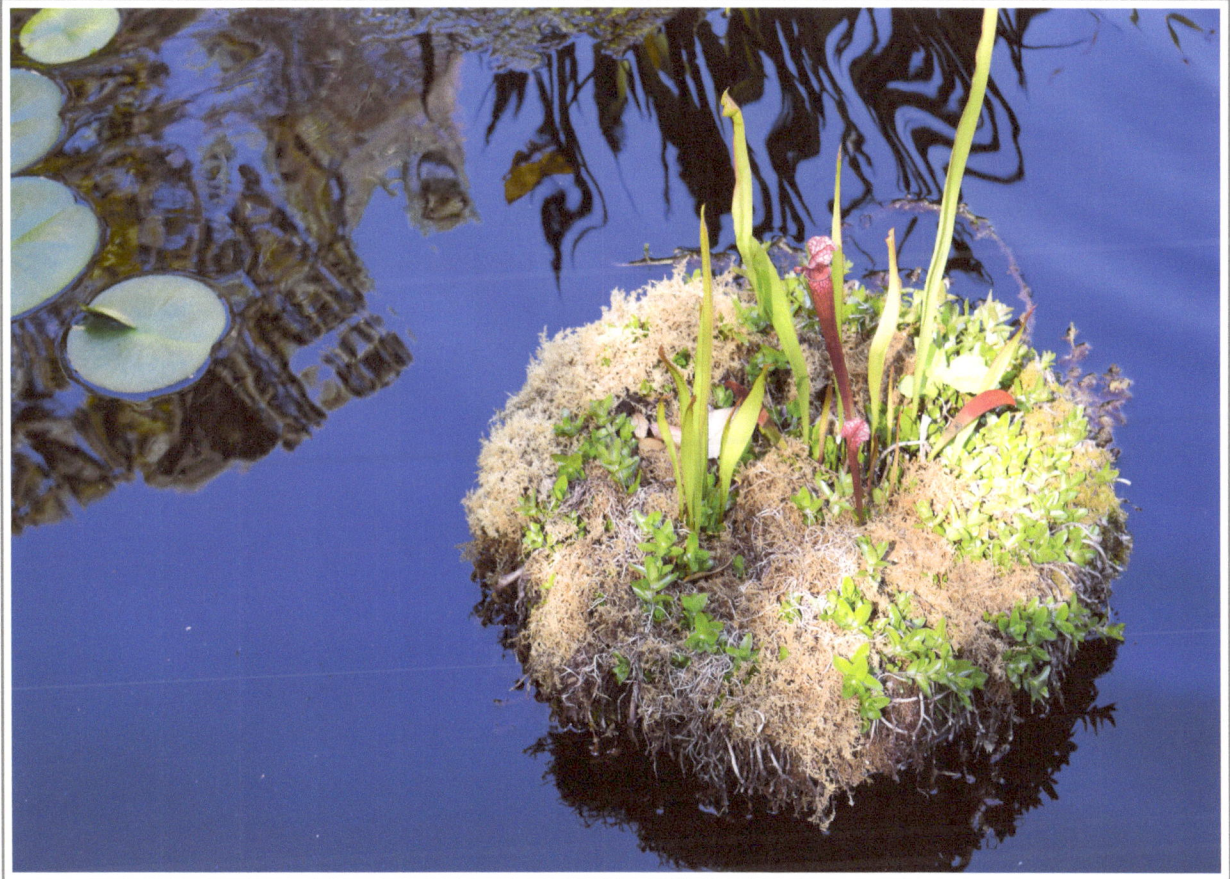

The Nature of Life Collection
Radical Reclamation Series • True Identity Project

I Am Kind and Loving

Once I believed a lie. I believed that I was unkind and uncaring.

I believed it when people said I did not care and judged me for claiming anything but a caring expressed in the way they most wanted to receive. I believed the lie that I was cold and had lost the ability to love. I believed it when the Prince of Darkness whispered to my broken spirit that I would never find the capacity for kindness and that I did not know its meaning.

Once I believed a lie. But now I know the truth of my identity.

The Spirit of the Living God has breathed a fresh wind of promise upon my life. I was blind, but now I see. The truth has been revealed: I am kind and compassionate, caring deeply about the world and those I meet within it.

Set free from the chains of a lie that bound me, I am restored to true identity.

True Compassion
"The Heart's True Friend"

The Nature of Life Collection
Radical Reclamation Series • *True Identity Project*

I Am Easy to Be With

Once I believed a lie. I believed that I was difficult. At home and away, at work or at play, I was called a problem, child of challenge.

I believed I made things complicated and knew nothing of the simple truths. I believed it when the Prince of Darkness whispered to my broken spirit that I would never cut through the clutter and return to true simplicity and ease.

Once I believed a lie. But now I know the truth of my identity.

The Spirit of the Living God has breathed a fresh wind of promise upon my life. I was blind, but now I see. The truth has been revealed: I am easy and choose simplicity. I am easy to get along with and put others at ease as I walk with grace and faith.

Set free from the chains of a lie that bound me, I am restored to true identity.

True Simplicity

"Walking on Sunshine"

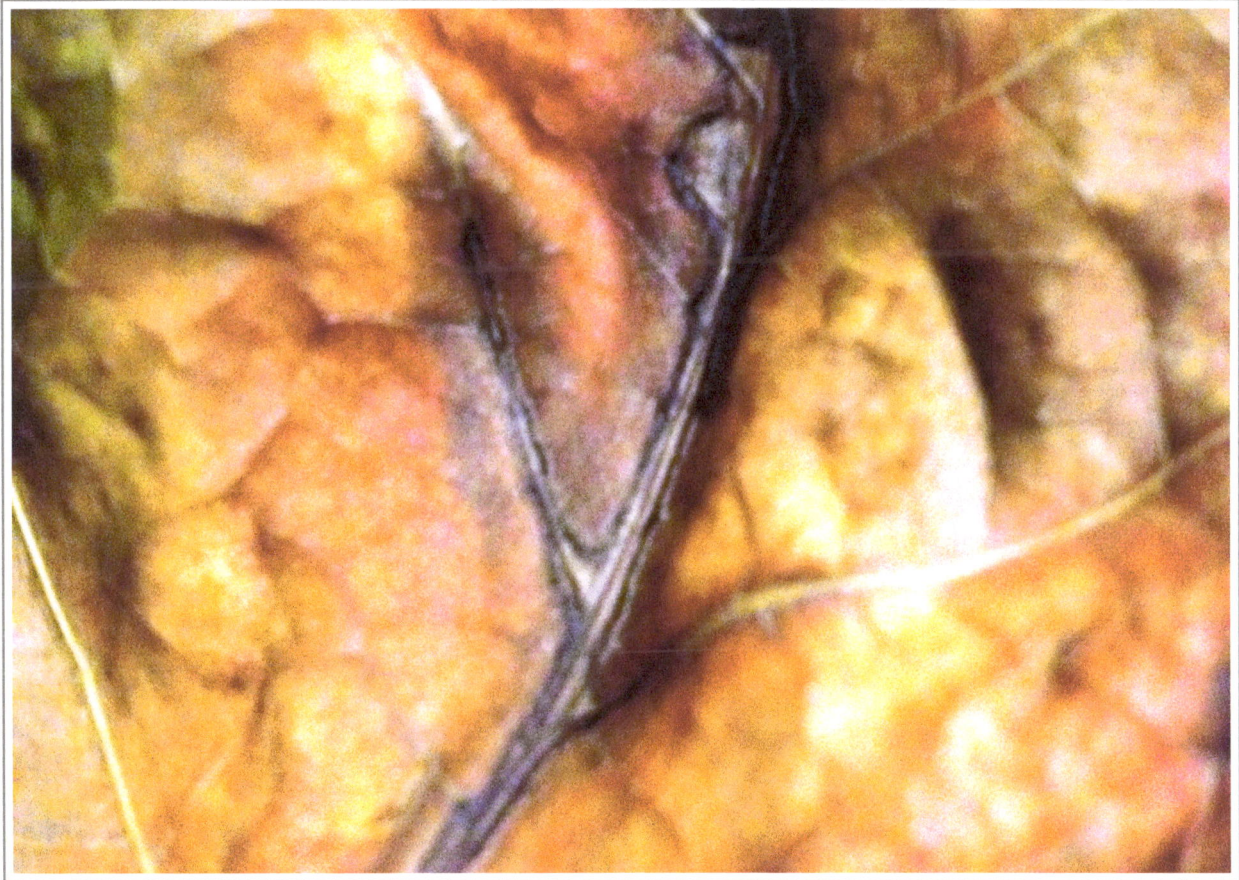

The Nature of Life Collection

Radical Reclamation Series • True Identity Project

I Am a Jewel Beyond Compare

Once I believed a lie. I believed I was null and void, without value, worthless in this world.

I believed it when they said nothing I had to offer was anything they or anyone would desire. I believed it when the Prince of Darkness whispered to my broken spirit that I was irredeemable and devoid of virtue, without hope of repair and with no way to make up for the total loss I was.

Once I believed a lie. But now I know the truth of my identity.

The Spirit of the Living God has breathed a fresh wind of promise upon my life. I was blind, but now I see. The truth has been revealed: I hold this treasure of who I am as one with my Creator and this will not be taken from me. I am a jewel beyond compare, of inestimable value.

Set free from the chains of a lie that bound me, I am restored to true identity.

True Value
"Freedom Finds Her Home"

The Nature of Life Collection
Radical Reclamation Series • True Identity Project

I Am Fully Equipped to Thrive

Once I believed a lie. I believed that I was wholly incapable of learning how to live.

I believed I was hopeless when it came to all things practical and especially in love and money, in friendships and career. I believed it when the Prince of Darkness whispered to my broken spirit that I was destined for doom here on this earthly plane and bound to an eternal incapacity.

Once I believed a lie. But now I know the truth of my identity.

The Spirit of the Living God has breathed a fresh wind of promise upon my life. I was blind, but now I see. The truth has been revealed: I am capable of taking practical steps to reorder my life and enjoy full thriving through health, wealth, and happiness. All I need is given by God, who is my source and my supply.

Set free from the chains of a lie that bound me, I am restored to true identity.

True Capability
"Suspended in Grace"

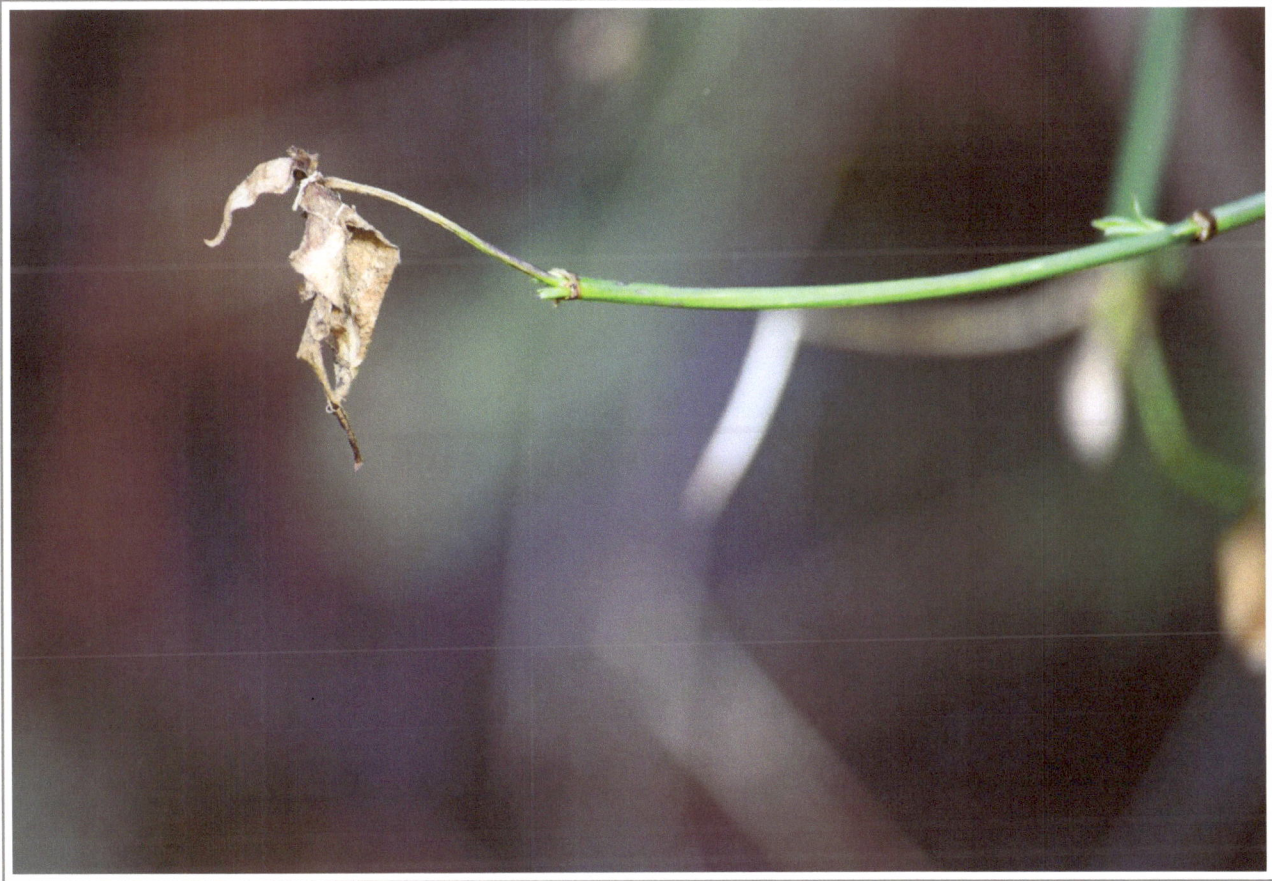

The Nature of Life Collection
Radical Reclamation Series • True Identity Project

An Invitation

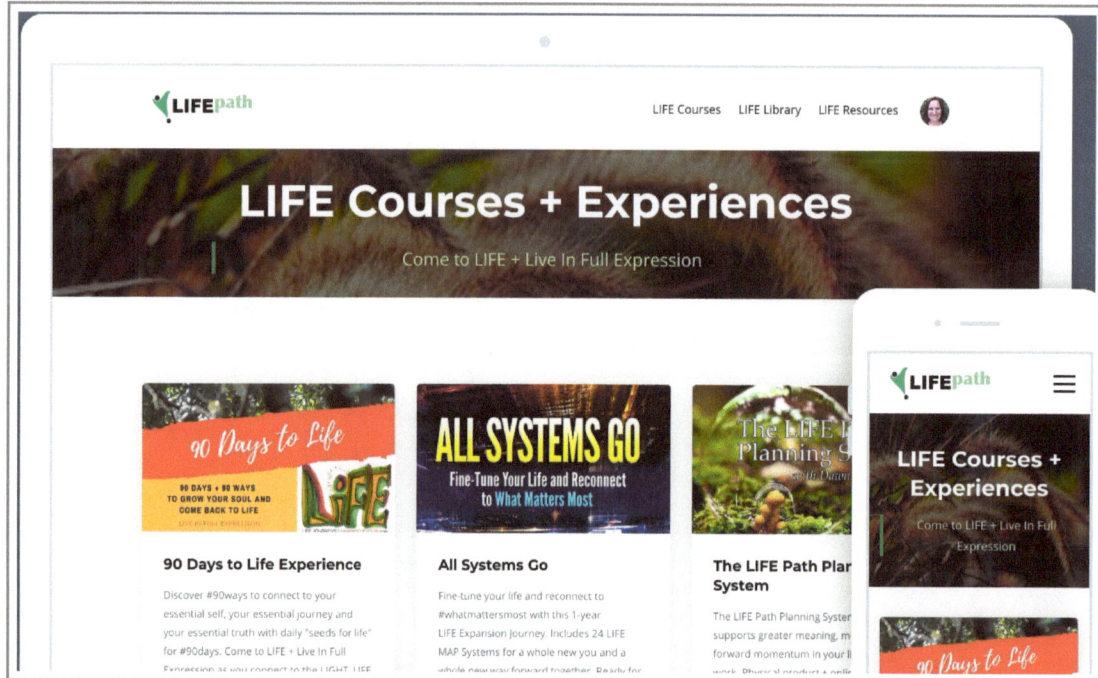

Meet me in the **Life Path Online Learning Center**
for life courses, journeys, and experiences to support you in full thriving
as you come to LIFE + Live In Full Expression,
expanding radiantly in life and life's work.

Look for the "**True Identity**" life course!
http://bit.ly/LIFEpathJourneys

About the Author

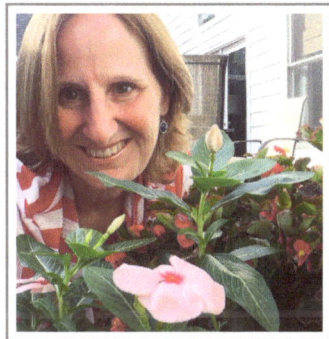

Dawn Richerson is founder of the Life Path Online Learning Center (http://bit.ly/LIFEpathJourneys) and CEO of Creative Revolutions Inc. Dawn also offers soulful, strategic support to bring Your Extraordinary Book to life. The creator of Lifeseeds, a core curriculum for LIFE + Living In Full Expression, Dawn is an author, artist, and photographer whose creative offerings connect you to your essential story of life. Learn more at DawnRicherson.com.

More Books from the Soul for the Soul from Dawn Richerson

- **SEEDS FOR LIFE** *The Lifeseeds Curriculum for Living In Full Expression*

- **ALL SYSTEMS GO** *Fine-Tune Your Life and Reconnect to What Matters Most*

- **AWAKENING THE WORLD WITHIN** *Cultivating Essence from the Matrix of Soul*

- **JOURNEY TO THE HEARTLAND** *A Spiritual Memoir on Life and the Desire for It*

- **JOURNEY TO SACRED WHOLENESS** *A Memoir on Healing and Grace*

- **SACRED PARTNERSHIP** *7 Pillars for the Radical Redefinition of Relationship*

- **A RECONCILIATION OF LIGHT** *Soul of Ireland Photographs*

- **BIRDS OF A FEATHER** *33 Essential Qualities for Thriving Together*